AS IS ENOUGH

A Poet Version of Myself

David Moneymaker

Copyright © 2022 David Moneymaker

All rights reserved

The characters and events portrayed in this book are fictitious. Any similarity to real persons, living or dead, is coincidental and not intended by the author.

No part of this book may be reproduced, or stored in a retrieval system, or transmitted in any form or by any means, electronic, mechanical, photocopying, recording, or otherwise, without express written permission of the publisher.

ISBN-13: 9798365216501
ISBN-10: 1477123456

Cover design by: Art Painter
Library of Congress Control Number: 2018675309
Printed in the United States of America

*For my friends
and myself*

CONTENTS

Title Page
Copyright
Dedication
Preface
Friends   1
Animals   13
Perception   30
Contemplation   47
Self   53
Summer   58
Autumn   63
Winter   73
Free Verse   79
Acknowledgement   85

PREFACE

These poems were written between April and November of 2022. Their ordering is not chronological, and no one poem is limited to the one category it happens to be placed in, my favorite example being "Helping my friends," which could be in three of the eight categories.

Each page is mostly blank thanks to the extremely short form of haiku. I want to encourage anyone who reads this to write in the pages, do anything with it. Use this book as a journal; change my poems, replace my words; draw on the pages; take notes for class or meetings; tear it out and write a note for someone; do anything with it!

FRIENDS

Early summer night;
      one host, thirteen guests.
  So much eye contact!

Before our show:
     something frivolous—funny—
  my friend studies hard.

Walking to campus;
 the couple jumps at my sight,
 then grins—morning fog.

Baking with a friend.
    Different work, same sweetness—
sweet as cherry pie.

Air conditioning,
> strong coffee making me shake.
> A friend brings stillness.

Brothers sit together
     searching for the right words
  in their coffee mugs.

After rain and hail
       the sun offers his love.
    A coffee break with friends.

Recalling a friend:
    "Trying not to stare down there,"
  in the coffee shop.

After a summer:
> lemonade—coffee—making;
see you around, friend.

With my friends:
    I remind myself
  how lonely I am.

Sometimes friends need
      to be strangers,
   again.

ANIMALS

Don't worry, ants,
      I guard this blanket
   for us.

Don't worry, Spider,
    you may reside on my porch
  until I am scared.

A mossy bird's nest
       made for a family of two
   on my porch.

In a stranger's yard
     under the shade of a tree—
  hummingbird, resting.

Under the shade of a tree
    my cat sleeps
   on a cool stone.

Helping my friends,
    the cat watches us, window-side.
  Downstairs autumn haze.

My cat squints
     trying to meet my gaze—
  summer light.

Under the pear tree—
    moths kissing our faces.
  Pockets filled with work.

Under the birch tree
     small bugs dance on our faces.
  Waiting 'til ev'ning.

In the sunflower patch:
    a rabbit enjoys the sunset
  with us.

Next to my right foot:
    enjoy our blues concert,
  Summer Azure, you.

Orange butterfly
     struggling against the wind,
  do you want to move?

Reading alone.
    Behind me:
  an anxious squirrel.

Two squirrels
 racing each other up a tree,
 pass me twice.

Two squirrels
> chasing one another,
> playing hide-and-seek!

Passing a person
      and her happy dog.
  I am a stranger.

PERCEPTION

What a brave lady,
	sitting so high above us:
   the moon at midday.

Sad Beauty?
   The morning glory painted without love,
  even.

Cresting the hill:
    the mushrooms are tired,
  too.

Unshaded by the trees,
 my book intervenes.
 "Everything stays."

Sun on my face:
    a warm blessing, in my eyes—
disruptive beauty.

Overgrown succulents
    mingle with my hair.
  One drunk family.

Digging in,
>   slowly wearing off the paint,
> my shoes—my fingers.

Interrupts my words,
> escapes my tight throat—a burp.
 Blushing through my hands.

Looking at the calendar—
	the present is inviting,
   too.

Days passing
      with little nothings—
   many of them.

In their custom golf cart:
    policemen—
  how boring.

Sitting on the ground,
      silenced by a busy mouth:
  "yummy food."

The coffee shop,
 greetings, again;
 familiar things change…

One happy matcha,
      a chai latte, happy, too!
  Thankful for the rain.

Strangers by default?
   Strangers by choice? It seems not.
  Lovers by design?

The stranger's laughter—
    familiar to my heart.
  Maybe he noticed?

CONTEMPLATION

Celebrate your love;
> give thanks to those who love you.
> Both can be a gift.

Having less than a dollar:
    almost a panhandling monk—
  almost desirable.

Looking for
      a home—some place—
  to die.

Jumping soul-first into Heaven:
   "To Heaven with Hell!"
  Who wouldn't be the wiser?

Hand sores:
    itchy robes of
  a modern guy.

SELF

I waste my time
      between the words
  we might share.

The coffeeshop plants;
>   drinking with the rest of us
today.

All the iced drinks
     prepared by our sticky hands—
  farmers market morning.

If you knew me,
    would we change,
  too?

SUMMER

Noisy and whining,
 restless in the summer—
 my electric fan.

Without summer pajamas
    I sleep uncovered—unrestricted—
  sticky with sweat.

Relentless heat
 making us talk about sweat,
 a casual conversation.

Embracing the bright sun,
    my brown shades
  sit at home.

AUTUMN

Brewed coffee in hand,
>   eyes stuck on the computer:
> "when it rains it pours…"

October rains
     gifting gratitude.
   Thanks be to them!

October rains falling,
 falling; kissing me—
  I'm kidding.

Midnight autumn chill—
    light rays arch into the sky.
  Miming a smoke break.

O kind autumn breeze,
    even lying in the sunlight
  can you chill my bones.

I've heard this
     same wind—same melody—
  through older trees.

How I missed your touch,
    so gentle and inviting—
  October wind.

October morning:
    all the leaves fell
  overnight.

Deeper into autumn—
    the moon begins to hide,
  again.

WINTER

These vigilant leaves
     and me, too:
   continually chilled by the wind.

Cold wind
    kissing my face.
  My eyes brim with tears.

Alone a dew,
> surrounded by this cold air;
> my hands will go numb.

Preparing to climb—
     bare feet on the forest floor;
   winter chill victims.

Approaching the cold season:
    driving into the sun
  hurts a little more.

FREE VERSE

Look into my eyes
and speak to me what you sense:

A presence of something
    —perhaps beyond what you and I are familiar with—
Yet this something is known to us.

Beauty,
    in my eyes, a reflection,
    you, and yours.

Touch my heart
And speak to me what you hear:

A sound of something
    —Certainly familiar to both you and I—
Yet this something is unknown to us.

Beauty,
    within my heart, a beating,
    you, and yours.

A presence of affection;
a sound of love.

When severed,
the ties we rely on
for love:
> Stability; Knowledge; Interest
> Faith; Hope; Sorrow
> Ache; Frustration; Grief
> Challenge; Encumbrance; Growth

they bind us to someone new.

We, not expendable,
seek to depend on others.
Community is human nature.
Absence will be filled.
Absence ought to be filled.

> Do not stand in the past and weep.
> We are not there.

Rejoice,
In life
And love:
> The life of love
> The love of life,

people!

When severed,
persevere, people!

O, my most loving wind,
Who has angered you?
Why do you now push me away?
When did your embrace become full of enmity?

This winter will be harsh.

O, my most inviting sun,
Who has hidden you?
Why do you now sleep all day?
When did your grace ruin me?

This winter will be unforgiving.

O, my most luxurious rain,
Who has changed you?
Why do you now conceal my way?
When did your pace relax to a mosey?

This winter will be harsh.
This winter will be unforgiving.

A man with a hiking bag
    Walks in front of me.

  He slows his stride,
    but does not stop.
His hand and eyes fall to the ground.
    He lifts his hand,
      holding a healthy rose.
His face beams with affection.
    He resumes his original pace,
      now accompanied with the rose.

The man with a hiking bag
    Walks out of my sight.

Anger, hate, love, war, and spite
Out of the many and by their action,
Destroy our heart with all their might.
I've never braved the winter.

Brother, sister, where am I?
Hidden faces and words of indifference
Leaving me here, leaving me to die.
Why can't I brave the winter?

Snow, ice, wind, night, hail, and frost
Out of the clouds and by their action,
Destroy our frame at any cost.
I'm helpless in the winter.

ACKNOWLEDGEMENT

Thanks to the few who encouraged me to publish these poems and to all the people, strangers and friends alike, who were unknowingly my inspiration.

Made in the USA
Columbia, SC
05 December 2022